Blue Star

Barbara Presnell

Press 53
Winston-Salem

Press 53, LLC
PO Box 30314
Winston-Salem, NC 27130

First Edition

Cover design by Kevin Morgan Watson & Barbara Presnell

Lee Hall, "Umbria Fall Morning," 2015, Mixed Media Collage on Canvasboard, 8 x 10 inches, Bechtler Museum of Modern Art, Charlotte, North Carolina, USA. Copyright © 2015 by Lee Hall.

Printed on acid-free paper
ISBN 978-1-941209-44-8

for Will

Acknowledgments

Grateful acknowledgment is made to the editors of the following publications in which these poems or earlier versions of them appeared:

Appalachian Journal: "Before All Three Brothers Leave for War," "Copperhead," and "Hair Cutting"

Change Seven: "The Death of Col. McCollum," and "A Sparrow Hangs by the Neck at My Feeder"

Chariton Review: "Children of Malmedy," "The Dance," "The Day Cornelius Ryan Came To Our House to Interview My Father for *The Last Battle*," and "My Son Tells Me Goodbye"

Connotation Press: An Online Artifact: "Ellie's War," "Diphtheria Outbreak, August 1898," "Josiah, 13," "My Grandmother Works the Bean Rows," and "Nails"

drafthorse: "Papa Buys the Tin Lizzie on the Day Slim Returns"

Innisfree Poetry Journal: "Annie Gum Chum," "Between Rains," "Blue Star War Mother," "Mess," and "What Flutters"

IthacaLit: "Finding Fox Red"

The New Poet: "At the Florida Butterfly Garden"

Prime Number Magazine: "After Sleeping in a Field Outside Paris," "Slim Joins Up," and "Southern Railway to Camp Glenn"

storySouth: "After the Train Carries Her Son to War, She Walks the Other Children Home"

War, Literature, and the Arts: "How to Cuss in French"

Wild Goose Poetry Review: "My Son Comes Home"

"In the Kitchen, We String Beans" appeared in the chapbook, *Snake Dreams*, published by Nightshade Press. "Gull, Fallen," appeared online at NC Arts Every Day as part of the series, "NC Poets on 9/11." "My Son and I Fish for Bluegill" appeared in the chapbook, *Unravelings*, published by Longleaf Press.

"After Sleeping in a Field Outside Paris," "Slim Joins Up," and "Southern Railway to Camp Glenn" appeared in the anthology *Prime Number Editors' Selections, Vol. 4*, published by Press 53. "After the Train Carries Her Son to War, She Walks the Other Children Home" appeared in *The Southern Poetry Anthology Vol. VII: North Carolina*, published by Texas Review Press. "Memorial Day, My Son Leaves Home" appeared in the anthology *Kakalak 2006: An Anthology of Carolina Poets*. "After He Registers for the Draft, My Son and I Hike Pilot Mountain" appeared in *Kakalak 2008: An Anthology of Carolina Poets*.

I am deeply indebted to my father, Bill Presnell, for saving an old army trunk so his children could find it and, in doing so, find him. Appreciation and love go also to my brother, Edwin Presnell, and my sister, Ellen Presnell Smoak, for joining me on a trek across Europe, following his footsteps, and to husbands David and Bill who patiently endured the journey. These poems have benefitted immeasurably from the generous critiques of readers, including Barbara Conrad, Mike Lewis-Beck, Rebecca McClanahan, Susan Laughter Meyers, Gail Peck, Diana Pinckney, and Dede Wilson. To Robin Greene, who keeps me on task, I owe many years of thanks. To Lee Hall and Carolyn Cozier for perfect cover art, I am deeply grateful. Much gratitude goes to Kevin Morgan Watson for his big spirit and his tireless service to the written word as well as his excellent guidance on this book. For the love and support of Bill, Will, and Mary Ellen, I am forever blessed.

Note: While the poems in this collection are based on family events and historical documents, the characterizations, dialogues, and stories are creations of the poet's imagination and are not intended to represent the actual experiences or feelings of the individuals.

Contents

III

*It is dark to-night, and over the plains of ocean
the autumnal sky rolls up the winter stars.*

—Henry Beston

Gull, Fallen

The blue fishing line trails from his mouth like spit,
dark pearls of eyes peering into dunes,
his beak opening and closing around hot sand.

My son, stopped in his run,
wraps his hands around the white-white breast,
folding wiry legs into soft gray wings.

I pinch the cut line and prod the narrow bill
open with thin driftwood.
There is no blood, only the pink cartilage

of his throat that wattles in his mouth.
He does not snap at me, no matter
how hard I tug the line from side to side,

but swallows and swallows around
the pronged trinity that has snagged
his ordinary afternoon. Maybe he dived

into surf where a fish wiggled, unaware
it was already caught. Maybe the fisherman
never knew what he hooked. *A big one,*

he'll tell his friends. *Broke the line clean off.*
A few feet away small pipers circle,
poking crabs and cooing. *There's nothing*

we can do, my son says. *We're making it worse.*
We lay him on a dune, shaded by sea grass.
His heavy head flops into sand.

That evening at dusk, we find him there still,
eyes fixed on the sea, a visitation of small tracks
wreathing his body, tide climbing in.

I

Copperhead

Last furlough before shipping out, 1943

At least he has the wits
to whack it with the shovel,
and pin its head against the porch step.
Pain like a gunshot streaks up his arm,
now swollen and blood red.
He snatches the handkerchief from his back pocket,
wraps it tight around his arm with his teeth
and collapses. It's his brother who

sucks and spits, sucks and spits
then hauls him in the car to the doctor,
carcass slung in the trunk.
Where there's one there's another,
everybody knows, so later that day,
his arm big as a leg, the prick
of the one tooth that got him
scarlet as sunset, ache in his whole body

almost more than he can bear,
he rakes everything clear of the house,
leaves, sticks, brush, whatever is bunched
and rotting there. He knows
the sons of bitches could be anywhere,
any size. He imagines them in the cellar,
curling beneath the kitchen, crawling
inside walls of the house. He can't

step outside without seeing them in the shrubs,
at the creek bed, on the street
headed downtown. They slither
through his dreams, their brass bodies coiling,
tongues splintering. Even in his bedroom,
where he fumbles at the collar
of his uniform, he sees them, crouching
in the corner, lying in wait by the door.

Before All Three Brothers Leave for War

They're on the front porch, shucking field peas,
chucking empty shells into buckets, peas into pans.
Their hands are green with pulp.

Mama's got the girls in the kitchen
where water's boiling hard and clean jars
are ready for packing and sealing.

Tom starts it. He pulls a hollow reed from his pocket,
stands behind the post and spit-shoots
onto Bill's bare arm. A pea-size welt rises.

Bill balances two at a time on a stick and flings.
Charlie picks up a fistful and lets them fly.
Pretty soon the purple peas are scattered across the porch

and strewn into front yard grass.
Later this afternoon, Mama will be furious,
will have them crawling on their knees,

picking up peas, saying, *You won't go anywhere*
until every single one is in my hand.

Blue Star Mother

Her oldest boy Slim, too old for war,
brings her the box he calls *radio*—
thick wood cabinet with knobs and a grill,

wires he strings through the doorway
of the bedroom to the kitchen.
He says, *Turn this button here, Mama.*

You can listen to President Roosevelt
and reporters across the ocean
talking about what all we're doing

to win this war. Sometimes she gets
a letter from Bill. *Can't tell you anything*
I don't know myself, he'll write.

Tom sends clippings from *Stars and Stripes*
with notes in the margin: *We were here*
or *Me and the boys were in on this one.*

From Charlie, nothing.
Three blue stars in her front window.
Every night before bed,

she shuffles to the window
where one by one she walks her finger
around the edge of each one,

feels the coarse fabric, the uneven stitch.
At breakfast, she stares at the box as though
her boys are inside. *You got to turn it on, Mama,*

Slim tells her, pulls a chair beside hers,
turns the knob, and static worse than
dying chickens screams out then settles.

After the Train Carries Her Son to War,
She Walks the Other Children Home, 1917

The baby rides on her back
like a rucksack, his sticky hands clinging
to her neck, her fingers
around his fat ankles.
The children are marching,

long sticks against their shoulders, leaves
on their heads for helmets.
At home she'll feed them cornbread
and milk, put the little ones down for naps
while she stirs a blackberry cobbler.

Supper will be like any other night.
Stew, kale, turnips, the cobbler,
its juices running down their chins,
their shirts, stains
she'll Borax out tomorrow.

More blackberries in the field,
she'll tell them, *and I'll need your help.*
More berries than she knows
what to do with. Not enough buckets
in the whole world to hold them all.

Memorial Day, My Son Leaves Home

Not long after he has pulled out of the driveway and gone,
I walk by myself to the courthouse square
where a small group has gathered, some circling
the monument to the Confederate dead,
others seated in plastic folding chairs
opened in formation along the Main Street curb.
A light mist has begun to fall. At the microphone
a man in a red VFW jacket reads from an unfolded paper,
his mouth so close to metal his words muffle.
I stand back from the group
because I am not a veteran or the wife of a veteran
just a daughter of one long gone and the mother
of a boy I pray will never see a battlefield.
To my right is a man whose gray hair collapses
at his shoulders. His ragged beard, his tarnished skin
and milky eyes say, *Vietnam, Vietnam,*
scream it into this quiet moment.
As each wreath of war is lowered to the ground,
I imagine that my son must have passed
through Raleigh by now, must be driving east
beside new tobacco fields and corn just beginning
to green up from the earth. Seven muskets
fire three times, their smoke
blending into fog. Then *Taps.* Beside me,
standing at attention and saluting the damp air,
the gray vet cries. As the bugle's
echoes fade, I imagine an arm, strong and brown,
resting in an open car window,
a shirt sleeve flapping in the wind.

My Grandmother Works the Bean Rows

East Bend, NC, 1890

No clouds in this July sky,
and sun tarnishes her brassy skin.
Her hornet black hair is ribboned
at her neck and washing
down her back, over shoulder bones

that move in rhythm with her digging.
She turns at the intrusion of a horse's hooves,
the impatient snort of the nag now bending
toward the fence, and the man, Josiah,
who has stopped to watch. Rising up

in his saddle, straight as the ladder back of a chair,
he tips his hat brim, smiles, says,
You really Injun like they say?
Her mother dead, her father gone, she belongs
to no one but Aunt Margaret with her own

dark-skinned children. This man who pauses at the field—
every single day—thick, fair hair, tall as she is,
hands coarse from smithwork and blistered
by scorching iron. What she ought to do
is curl her fingers around this clod of red clay

and skip-rock his face. What she does
is close her hand around a grin,
and when he says, *Wanna ride with me
to town and back?* she lays down
her hoe and climbs on.

In the Kitchen We String Beans

They mound like a grave on today's front page,
covering the news that a soldier was hanged,
strung up like a ham, in some faraway country.
My mother, my grandmother, my aunt, me.
We snip heads from beans,
unthread their sides then snap the green flesh
into finger joints we'll cook for supper.

I listen as they talk of cancer,
how suddenly it comes, how quickly it works,
how Herbert Combs planted his corn
on the slant of his hill two weeks
before he died, how old Ethel,
thin as a vine this Sunday at church,
won't last long.

The soldier's smiling face peeks at me
through beans in my pile. His newsprint eyes
dampen with dew that came in from the garden.
His skin softens. He is a boy,
my son's age, arms and legs
like tender pods, plucking beans
from stems before the season
takes them to seed.

We are a family of women
who grow older than oaks.
Every summer, we string beans,
slicing out the imperfections
with a blade. Grandmother strings
slowest of us all, for beans slip
between her thick fingers too often
for speed.

I am waiting to die, she told me
two nights ago. Now she says
how good these beans will taste
with a spoonful of grease and a
bite of cornbread.

Ellie's War

Little River, 1861

This one, Josiah, on the floor at her feet.
At the table, that one scribbling on a slate.
Curtis at the Meeting House with the others,

deciding, and her in this dark candle-thick house
with the children, pondering for herself his choices:
Does he join up? If not, he runs or takes his gun

to the woods to live till this is over. Who'll then
be left to papa these girls? These boys?
That one, stirring gravy in the kitchen?

That one, stacking sticks at the hearth?
Curtis says he won't go, conscript or no.
No money to buy his way out like some others,

not with these younguns and so little rain.
Won't go to jail, won't run like a rabbit.
If they come for him, well, we'll see, by God.

Not our war, he says. Then why, she wants to know,
are blue coats camped out in our field,
are gray boys killing neighbors like dogs?

A shuffle out the window, leaves unsettling
but there's no wind tonight. She's got the rifle, has
an eagle eye. This one on the floor, hungry, starts to cry.

Quaker Boy

So close he can see the heartbeat
in the squirrel's leg. He shifts his sight
to the muscly chest, tightens
his finger on the trigger, thinks,

meat on the table tonight.
A jabber in the trees, a rustle. He turns,
expecting deer or another squirrel
but what he sees is blue, brass-buttoned,

dark as a woolen sky. He lowers
his barrel, doesn't breathe.
This one now on Papa's land,
likely stealing from Papa's field.

No telling how many more out there
or how many gray coats, faces
they know—Jimmy Perl, Franklin Lowe,
the Cox twins—boys who have eaten

at Mama's table, slept beside him
in the woods. Back at the house,
children grow hardy as turnips.
When the little ones sleep, he watches

out the window, thinks about going,
imagines himself skirting among trees,
wonders what it'd be like killing
folks he never had battle with

because of the color of their coats
or the way their mouth crooks
around a word. He follows
this one with his rifle, on through

brush to the creek, bent down
for water, on through new corn—
a clean shot—into the wheat field
amber and ready for harvest.

Josiah, 13

Little River, 1874

Picture him, hair cast in sun
and thick as hay, a tall boy, paused
by his horse at the edge of a field to gaze

out toward the woods and beyond.
August heat scorches down on late summer corn,
tasseled and plumping for harvest.

He doesn't know much beyond this acreage,
can't imagine himself next year,
let alone one day with a girl by his side,

and children as measured as kernels on a cob.
All he knows is the trouble he'll find
if he isn't home soon but he doesn't

think about that. He doesn't think at all,
but feels—his bare chest, hips tucked
into loose britches, too tight boots

passed down from his brothers, brown skin
prickling, cheek flush and warm against
the sweaty neck of his bay.

Diphtheria Outbreak, August 1898

... the strangling angel of children ...
—from *The Lancet,* 1859

In the dark, too-hot house, Hannah rocks
Clifton—already Josiah calls him Slim,
not much fat on his five-year-old bones.

He struggles to breathe, his body so scalding
her skin burns. Germs all around,
but she can't see them, couldn't see

when they stole into Blanche the baby,
taken on Tuesday, or three-year-old Nellie,
this morning gone.

Clifton thrashes and cries, croaky and sharp-edged.
Beside her sits the bucket of water
Josiah brought before he left with Nellie's body.

Squeeze of her arm, a whisper, *He's strong.*
He can fight it. Can he? She dips a cloth in,
washes his face, his chest,

his arms. His legs hang
over her elbow's bend, his head sags.
Her full breasts ache for the baby Blanche

they don't yet know is gone. The still air whispers
Nellie. But now, this skinny, dark-haired boy,
too much life in him to soften into sleep.

Nails

Tonight in the shop by lantern light
and fire, Josiah saws and measures
pine boards for a box. Twenty-one inches,
head to heel, plus one hand-width on either end.

Eighteen at the shoulders,
narrowed to nine at her feet.
Get the body in the ground today,
says Doc Burton. *Children are dying*

all over town. Josiah knows
what he means, his boy at home
with fever hot as the furnace
he works in. His brother Dan says,

Dovetail it. Take your time and do it well.
Perfect joinery for perfect child.
But on this anvil he himself forged the iron lengths
now cooling in his palm, one fist around the tongs,

one clutching the hammer, strength of his arm
pounding the fiery rods to draw them out
true and sharp enough to penetrate
the toughest wood, right enough

for the red and yellow quilt
Hannah stitched in her seventh month
that will line the box and fold around
the toes, face, small shock of steel-black hair.

Skin Color

You really Injun like they say?
—Josiah, 1890

When dark-skinned men would knock
on the back screen door—kitchen door that opened
to her garden and the well where the children pumped water—
when they'd stand on the bottom step and ask Josiah,
Is there work? he'd holler back to where Hannah stood

in her apron, stirring beans or frying a skillet of ham,
and say, *Your cousins are here to see you.*
Furious then for a week or more,
she would talk to him only through the children
and lock the bedroom door. He'd sleep

on the slatted front porch rocker.
Finally she'd warm to him, say,
*When I get my Indian money, you won't
be laughing,* and off they'd go in the buggy,
leaving the oldest in charge.

By the time the government letter
did arrive, without a check,
he was head to boots in blacksmith soot,
and she milked and floured to her elbows
from okra sizzling on the stove.

Eastern Cherokee Application # 13598

*For share of money appropriated for the Eastern Cherokee Indians
by Act of Congress approved June 30, 1906, in accordance with
the decrees of the Court of Claims of May 18, 1905, and May 28, 1906*

Jan. 28, 1907

Dear Mr. Guion Miller,
Betty Pledge my Great-Great Grandmother was said to be a
daughter or granddaughter of Donnahoo a Cherokee Chief whose
tribe was located in Surry County, NC, at a point now named
Donnaha, NC. I claim through my mother Eliza Webb, daughter of
Hannah Webb, daughter of John Poindexter whose wife was Betty
Pledge. Please send my money directly to me in East Bend, NC.
Respectfully yours,
Hannah Sharpe

June 3, 1907

Dear Mr. Guion Miller,
No, sir, my mother did not apply because she is deceased and
my father who is not a rightful descendant is also deceased. I
have four living children and I reckon if I get my money then
they are entitled to some as well, being that they are half mine.
Please send my money to me at my residence in East Bend, NC.
Respectfully,
Hannah Sharpe

August 21, 1907

Hello again, Mr. Guion Miller,
I only have one name that I have ever been told and that is
Hannah Anne Sharpe so for your record you can put that down as my
English name and my Indian name. I am still in East Bend waiting.
Yours truly,
Hannah Anne Sharpe

Dec. 31, 1907

Dear Mr. Miller,
Sir, has my application 13598 been examined and do you

need any more information. I can get all that is necessary to prove I am a descendent from the Eastern Cherokee tribe.

Sincerely,

Hannah Anne Donnahoo Sharpe

Jan. 31, 1908

Guion Miller, Special Commissioner,

I do not agree with your decision because I have been told all my life that I was Indian and I will prove it to you if you will come here to East Bend and see for yourself. I meant to tell you Donahoo was suppose to be part of the Snowbird clan which now is pretty big if you consider that all us Poindexters belong to it and we are all over the county. I would like for you to rethink your action and all of us here in East Bend feel the same.

Awaiting your reply,

Hannah Anne Donnahoo Poindexter Sharpe

Feb. 25, 1908

Dear Commissioner:

I am a Christian as well as Indian and whatever your people in Washington say I know who I am and where I come from. One day right will win out. You mark my words.

Yours most sincerely,

Mrs. Hannah Anne Donnahoo Poindexter Sharpe

Mar. 13, 1908

Guion Miller—

No, sir, I do not mean to threaten you. I just want you to see the truth for yourself. There's nobody in East Bend who will hurt you. I don't think.

Signed,

Hannah Anne Donnahoo Poindexter Webb Sharpe
East Bend, N.C.

Slim Joins Up

May 1917

He'll tell Papa first,
how he climbed the steps above the grocery
to Armory Hall where this time
there was no dancing, no rummy, no liquor

brought in by county boys or the Reeves brothers
and nobody's sisters or cousins from Greensboro
in tight dresses with bobbed hair—
though their scent remained where groups

of boys like him gathered,
filling out papers, standing against height lines,
raising palms for oaths, making boasts
they swore they'd keep even if bullets

scraped their heads and their skin bloodied
but not with the blackberry juice of summer.
He'll tell Papa what Papa knows—
the Jerries in their brown uniforms,

children dying, evil rising up fast
as new corn. *Anyway, Papa,*
you know I'm not cut out for farming.
Papa won't cry like Mama will,

or grip his arm and turn her face away
Slim'll laugh and tell her chances are
they won't get called up anyway.
All we'll do is lay around and whine

for biscuits and your red eye gravy.
Anyway, what's done is done,
he'll tell them both.
He won't sleep that night,

will lie awake on the front porch cot,
watching clouds across a restless sky
as crickets murmur from the grass,
a lullaby of sorts, Mama would say.

18

II

After He Registers for the Draft,
My Son and I Hike Pilot Mountain

Because he is 18 and nothing
can hurt him, he leads.
We are walking the top of God's head,
the name he gave this knob
when he was too small to carry the pack
he now carries with water for us,
a Snickers bar each, the map.
Beside the Yadkin the narrow trail
bumps over roots and rock.
A group of horsemen sidles down to the river
and passes to the other side, crossing the current
as though they follow an invisible route.
Their horses do not hesitate, not even once.

My son tells me he has seen wild boars
so close he could hit them with a stick,
their teeth snagging on whiskers thick
as steel blades. He's been asleep
when elk have lain beside his tent,
heat from their bodies pressing against his.
Even bears have left blood
near his campfire. He's pretty much
seen it all in the woods, he tells me,
is not afraid of anything.

Suddenly he whips around,
spins my shoulders, pushes me back.
Go, he says, *go*, his face steeled and white.
When we finally stop, he says,
It was huge. Covered the path.
Head like a diamond. I'm lucky
I saw it before my boot came down.
There is an almost indecipherable
shiver in his voice, so small that
if I didn't know him so well
I would not detect it.
We sit on a fallen trunk

sharing bites of chocolate.
Overhead, a small dot of hawk circles.
He stares across the river where the horses have gone,
silent, and I can't take my eyes from him.

Mama's Boy

Slim stretches on the front porch cot,
watches clouds move across a dark
sky, smokes, one arm behind his head.
A hazy glow lifts from the girls' room and
the shadow of Ruth at the window

likely eyeing that same sky, planning
a life away from here. Beside her, Alma will be
sleeping, clenching the cloth dolls Mama made.
In the boys' room, Tom won't wake
when little Charlie wraps his muggy arms

around him or when Billy's hot body
presses into his. Jake lies alone
on the daybed downstairs.
Slim can't recall the two babies that died,
though now and then he'll see a leaf

curled around a twig and the idea
of a finger will come to him and the vague
recollection of a finger gone cold.
It's Mama's crying he can't forget,
him limp with fever, in and out

of sleep, barely five but old enough
to understand he couldn't leave her.
Same cry when he told her he'd joined up,
an animal sound, bobcat or coyote.
My children, Slim thinks, as much as they are

Mama's and Papa's, and he loves them all.
Through the screen door he hears
Papa's snore and a weeping he knows
will fill the house and bring him back no
matter what continent calls him away.

Southern Railway to Camp Glenn

He watches what passes by—a cow farm,
blackberries ripe in the briars, trees losing leaves,

trumpet vines clinging to summer, houses
with people who wave from porches, streets

where mothers are walking their babies
or hauling sacks of groceries. High Point.

Greensboro. Burlington. Durham. Headed east
where they say the earth is sand, water salty,

and the ocean stretches green and white
to the edge of the sky. Most these boys

he grew up with—Jack, Ernest, Walter, Hal.
Sat beside in school, hunted with, stole

their daddies' whiskey, got whipped
by their mamas' switches. Now row after row

in matching uniforms, nothing but a rucksack
with their name inked on, nothing but bragging

about things that don't matter now, if they
ever did. At home, his brothers and sisters

are probably eating corn bread and chicken pie.
He'll write to them about fields of peanuts

that run for miles, the ice-cold sea, and *I'm fine,
I'm good, all the boys excited, can't wait to get*

over there and end this thing. Train slowing down
to cross a road. *Almost in Raleigh*, somebody says,

the field out there brown with harvested wheat,
and he watches a white mutt

skirt around the stubs, digging for something,
snake or rabbit, that burrows underground.

Letters Home

August 21, 1918
France

My dearest darling,
You have asked me lots of times to tell you something about this country. I am in a place now where there is not a whole house standing together and lots of times you can see women and little children leaving their homes for a better place to stay. I am in a house tonight where there have been people living and it looks as if it had been a real fine home. But tonight there is nothing but about half of it standing. So you can imagine the condition this country is in.

Aug. 24, 1918
France

My dearest darling,
I am getting along all right. I like trench life fine, that is, I mean, for the period I am over here. I feel perfectly safe all the time for I do not feel that I will ever be wounded in battle, but I am coming back to you as safe as I was when I left you.
But the Hun's bullets are passing over us all the time. Some are falling all around us and some in front of us. Last night I went out of my dug out and just as I stepped on the outside, one of Jerry's large ones, what we call *whig bungs* busted within ten feet of where I was standing, and believe me I was covered with dirt and everything else that was on the ground.

Oct. 6, 1918
Gen Hosp # 73
England

My darling wife,
I know it has been some time since you have heard from me but please do not be worried now. If you haven't already heard about the battle Sunday morning, Sept. 29, that was the one we

were in. I was wounded by shrapnel fire in my neck just as we started over the top. I haven't heard yet what has become of my company or any of the boys. I don't know what has become of my brother Colon. When I left, there had been 8 men killed. Today I heard my captain was killed sometime that day. And today I heard that my company came out of the trenches with only 5 men and so it is with the rest of the companies.

O darling, you can't ever imagine what a battle we were in that morning. I don't see how any one lived through it and I certainly can thank God for sparing my life. I only hope that I may live to get back to you.

Yours only and forever,
Ernest

Between Rains

His rifle is steady
like he's got a bead on a deer
though nothing's ahead but the barbed wire
him and his fellows aim to break through.
Shoulder to shoulder on their bellies
against the wall of this trench,
the only sound some low-breathed prayers
and down the line a boy who can't stop crying.
At the order, they'll run like hell,
take what comes, try to give it back.
He's fast. Always could
outrace anybody in town. Skinny too.
If raindrops can't hit him, like his mama says,
maybe Huns' bullets can't either.
Some fellow passes a cigarette. He drags,
sends it down the line, not looking right or left
but into the purple-pink sky
where a bird circles, its occasional caw
cracking the dawn. It's all luck anyway,
he thinks, who you're born to, what country,
how tall, where you end up, when you die.
Goddamn bird, some fellow growls.
Goddamn flying bird.
Then the sharp whistle, the call,
and he scrambles with the rest of them
over the top, the mud, so much mud,
splattering on every part of him.

Premonition

What if Ruth had listened the night before she left,
a green moon piercing the upstairs window,
her hand around a fig stolen from the kitchen
when Mama turned her head. What if she had heard

the message in the cards her sister Alma spread,
You'll always wish you never left,
you won't come home again to stay,
Mama will never forgive you.

Alma's eyes were pulsing, and Ruth wondered
if it was really her sister at all—the little girl
who read too much, gave everything
a mother and father, did not yet have breasts

or understand anything except her brother
went to war, another brother followed, now
this sister she had shared a bed with all her life
was leaving, and nothing—not Ruth's sticky fingers

on the sill, not the wind that lifted her skirt
as she clambered down the trellis, not the green
moon, not the orange sky, not even the truth—
could make her stay.

Bus Station, 1919

In the checkered satchel Ruth packed
stockings, two clean dresses, underclothes and corset,
sleeping gown, hair brush, red ribbon, soap,
blue sweater, two years of wishing for this day,
an address scribbled on a napkin, powdery
scent of Mama's babies, sticky odor of boys, the ribbed
texture of her dreams, her heart pulsing
with a life she imagines, fourteen dollars
saved from working at the grocery every afternoon,
enough for a one-way ticket and a room somewhere.

A ticket flags from Slim's shirt pocket.
In the duffle at his feet is one dress uniform,
polish and a rag for shoes, army issue bvds,
drops for the eye that won't stop stinging,
picture of his girl, picture of his dog, a handful of francs,
the home addresses of six buddies and two mothers of buddies,
one government check, a crumpled pack of Camels,
things seen, heard, tasted he wishes he'd left behind,
vague memory of Mama's chicken pie, fear that when
he opens his own back door, no one will know who he is.

Papa Buys the Tin Lizzie on the Day Slim Returns

I will build a car for the great multitude.
                                    —Henry Ford

Slim brings home a limp
he got in France from shrapnel in his knee.
Flat tire, Papa calls it.
All you need is a little air. So he leaves his iron
and anvil in the shop, goes to Cox Motor Company,
hands over $480 cash, drives home a black

Model T Touring car, top folded back to a fan,
and says, *Get in, boy. We're going for a ride.*
Slim lays his cane across the back seat,
steps in. He's out of uniform and into
the old blue-checkered shirt Mama washed
and ironed when she heard he was coming.

I'm tired, he says. *But I'll take a short one.*
April sun careens down, a breeze
grabs hold of Slim's shirt sleeve, flapping it
like a sheet. They're not yet out of town
when Papa peels away the jacket
of his Sunday wool suit, rolls cuffs to his elbows.

If there'd been a radio, it would have
been blasting. Instead, just air whistling in,
an occasional gnat, the rumble-bump of tires
on tar and gravel, dirt, and sometimes grass or field.
Papa stops in front of Julian Barnes's corn,
gets out, stretches his legs, smokes.

Slim sits with the door open, stares
at the cows walking toward the fence,
moos at them a time or two, then says,
That's enough. Let's head home.
But Papa says, *Not yet.*
Out then beyond the county line

to a point where the Uwharrie opens so wide
all they see of the other side is the pinnacle of trees.
Catfish and yellow-green turtles splash the edges.
Dark is shifting in as they turn the Lizzie
toward the top of Shepherd's mountain
and settle on the hillside, where Slim sleeps.

When he cries out or shakes with terrors
Papa holds him like when he was a boy sick with fever.
Then morning and the reveille of birds.
Papa says, *Drive*, and even though
Slim's knee flames, he takes the wheel.
It's mid-morning by the time the Model T pulls in.

Papa's down to his undershirt, Slim's old
blue-checkered is unbuttoned all the way.
His arm hangs around Papa's shoulder,
the cane still in the back seat.
Two months later, Papa will change
the sign above his shop from *Blacksmith*

to *Automobiles* and learn the insides of an engine
like it's the machine of his own body.
Boys home from war will buy them like cheap
cigarettes, crowding streets, pushing buggies
to the sides, smoking up and down roads.
After that first day, only Slim will drive the Lizzie.

Sometimes Papa will climb in beside him.
Or Slim will get in by himself, not come home
till morning. Sometimes for days.
That wood cane never will leave the back seat,
though finally it will slip beneath the cushions,
only now and then catching a splinter of light.

The Viewing

After Jake's baby died of pneumonia, he held it up to the living room window so people could come by and pay their respects without catching anything from it. Everybody wanted to see the baby—blue-gray and puffed up like a fish—wanted to see if it looked like Jake or Imogene or neither, wanted to see what it looked like dead, Jake holding it up in its white burial dress, him smiling like it was the baby's baptism or coming out party, its eyes closed, fat little body stiff as a tree. Nobody asked if it was a boy or girl. Nobody asked its name. *Jake's baby*, they called it. *Three months and a day*. Never right. Born with small lungs is what they said, and when the pneumonia took hold, well, wasn't much anybody could do.

Mama had shoved the couch out of the way and faced a ladderback chair toward the window for Imogene so people could see her upset and crying, her being not from around here, and they wanted to be sure about her. Billy had never seen a dead baby, so he liked the whole thing, except Mama made him wear his church clothes, the collar which was tight around his neck and not comfortable at all. After he sat a while, speaking to the grownups like he was supposed to, Mama still wouldn't let him go outside with the boys, said even if the baby never did do anything but cry and make Jake cuss, it was family and he would pay his respects for as long as need be.

Then Mama had Billy on the front porch pouring tea for everybody, it being 95 degrees outside, and her figuring some women might be fading. Some wanted to linger and talk, which was fine, but Jake's arms were getting heavy holding that dead baby, and Papa said they had to hurry up and get it in the ground, it being August and everybody knows how fast stuff goes bad in August.

Saturday Serials

Starring Rin-tin-tin as The Lone Defender, *1930*

In March, Ruth sent her son Jack
on the train from Chattanooga to stay
with Mama and Papa till things got settled
but nobody said what needed to settle.
Jack's all the time talking to Billy about how

he's going home tomorrow or next week,
or *you just wait and see if I don't leave here
by Friday.* But it's August, he's still here, and
Mama went ahead and signed him up for third grade.
That night over supper, all the children

including Jack plus Mama and Papa.
They're chewing on their stew beef
when Mama says to Jack, *Got a letter
from your mama today.* Jack elbows Billy,
mouthing the words, *I'm headed home.*

Mama takes a knife bite of beef, continues.
She says not now. Maybe Christmas.
Everything seems to stop, nobody wanting
to look at Jack or let on that Mama
might as well have stabbed him instead

of her stew beef, him being only
nine years old and still loving his mama
to death no matter what. There's
no sound but ice clinking in glasses
and forks scraping across plates.

Jack's right cheek starts to tic then
his left but nobody sees it except Billy.
Papa *ahems* just to make some noise,
and Billy, looking everywhere now
but at Jack, in clear, round syllables

and in a voice loud enough to be heard
on the back side of the barn,
says, *Son of a bitch.*
Silence dead as Grandpa Curtis,
dead as Mama's two babies, nobody

thinking about Jack anymore but Billy
and what kind of trouble he's gotten
himself into, not a single one at the table,
not even Papa, brave enough to say a word
or glance at Mama who by now should have

one hand on the soap and another
on a switch, Billy's words lingering in the air
above the table till finally Mama says,
Pass the biscuits this away, Bill,
and Billy does and that is the end of it.

That was last night. Jack got a pocket full
of money in the letter from his mama and
he gave Billy a quarter—a full quarter. Now
three rows back, Billy sits watching Rin-tin-tin,
tearing the cover off his 5th Avenue bar,

finishing in two bites, reaching for the Zagnut
in his shirt pocket. Jack's beside him,
sucking on a Sugar Daddy. They're hooting
and cheering and neither one can sit still,
which doesn't matter because

nobody in the theater is quiet.
NEXT WEEK, CHAPTER 3: THE JAWS OF PERIL
rolls across the screen and it's over.
Billy and Jack push down the aisle and
into Saturday sunshine where Jack says

he'll buy Billy a co-cola and some ice cream
at the Little Castle before they go home.
Billy punches him in the arm because
that's what they do and says,
Yeah, I'll take that.

How to Cuss in French

July 1944

Army issue dictionary
thin as the soles of his boots

pulled off and lying in grass.
Ten-minute break, blister raw

on his right toe. He's stretched out,
helmet off, head on his bedroll,

studying words he should have learned
in school that now might mean the difference.

Américain! Je suis un ami!
Those days in back row French class,

staring out at the dusty ball field or
two seats up a girl's oaky brown hair,

what was there to do but scribble away
the long inside hours, inking boredom

in the margins and across his book's cover:
    How to Cuss in
    ~~*The Elements of*~~ *French*

Endless those days seemed, endless
these. It's here in the Normandy orchards

he's learned how to cuss: you put one foot
in front of the other and keep going.

After Sleeping in a Field Outside Paris

He yawns at the small annoyance
on his arm—leggy mosquito that hovers,
flits, hovers. Above him, the linen-green

leaves of an oak, acorns unbuttoning
from its limbs. White fence. A trumpet vine.
If he had a jar he'd scoop crawdads

from creek water tracing the meadow.
Crisp autumn air says a perfect day
for hunting—turkey, duck, deer, squirrel.

He's been dreaming himself back home
at the fair with a girl and his old dog Buck
that died last summer, dreaming

himself behind the pageant stand—
whatever her name was—her lips and his.
He jerks, slaps his arm, the mosquito falls,

and he touches the damp ground, his helmet,
boots heavy as stones. Looking up, he is blinded
by a fiery burst that is not sun.

Billy Graduates

At first he thinks anything is better
than endless afternoons of conjugations
and dissections inside a May classroom,
stuffed in a desk made for a little body,
sun burning down on his paper, his brain
scorched with a lifetime of school.
A week or two of lazing around,
then he starts at the mill. Day after day
on the freight dock, eight hours, twenty-
minute lunch, cigarette break every hour—
he's never smoked before, but now

he can't wait to light up. Graduated
to what? he wonders. One or two boys
headed off to college but not him.
Maybe his brother can get him on as a roofer—
but who wants July afternoons nailing shingles
when at least at the mill there's shade.
There's a girl in sewing from Ulah, slim
as a thread, hair rippled like creek water,
and he's got his eye on her. What else is there?
Trading desk for dock, teacher for boss,
money in his pocket, a future of nothing
but pack and load, pack and load.

Back Home

July 14, 1944

Dear Mama,
I sure did enjoy that last letter I got from you.
It sure did have a lot of news. You said that
Mrs. Ridge said Johnnie was somewhere
you couldn't remember just where.
That Mrs. Bunting had heard something about Albert
but she didn't say what it was. That you had heard
Larry Steed had some kind of scholarship
but you didn't know what kind it was and that
Bobby Steed was down somewhere going
to some kind of school and when he got through
he was going to some other kind of school
but they didn't give you the particulars.

Mama, I sure am glad you plan on
sending me a pound cake. I just hope you
put it in the box before you mail it.

Write soon.

Love,
your boy Bill

What Flutters

Heat rising. Tick of afternoon sun.
The screen door, banging. A telegram.
When it comes, Hannah is in the kitchen making dinner.
She slips her greased finger beneath the flap,
hands trembling so she can hardly read.
>   *Company almost wiped out. Stop. Our boys*
>   *fought bravely to the end. Stop.*
It's the *almost* she clings to as day splinters
into days, then a week.

Wings tipping. Grass that pillows.
Loose fabric. A place called France—she's seen it on a map
and Slim sent a postcard back in July.
Words. Picture of a cow in a field like theirs.
Bone jur scribbled above the cow's ear.
Seems like a fine place on the back side. And,
>   *Everybody says hi. I sure miss*
>   *your cold ice tea, Mama.*

Flotilla of red leaves. Fine hairs
of a sweet potato. Screen door
banging. Her husband Josiah holds the letter.
He's alive. Our boy. Then names those gone:
>   the Dixon's youngest, Jimmy Gatlin,
>   Big John Pugh. More.
His gray chin on her shoulder.
Dusk stirring in.

Josiah, 77

August 1938

Afternoon sun strikes his window
like a hammer on an anvil, shaping his last day.
He knows what he's made—ten children,

a life with one woman, all these years
with fire and iron, horseshoes, knives,
nails, hinges, axles. Now fever and chill,

fever and chill, an unfamiliar forging.
It's August. Hannah's set the fan, opened
shades, dampened his face with rags.

Town's oldest citizen, his obituary will read,
and *kept a shop till he was 75* and
two children preceded him in death.

He'll miss the next war, more grandbabies,
great-grandbabies bearing his name.
That oak out front will be hit by lightning

and topple on the roof, taking down the house.
The old dog will die and another and another
take its place. Hannah will live

thirty years without him, forgetting
everything before she dies.
He turns his head toward his watch that lies

on the nightstand, checks the time.
Another hour until nightfall. This day's fire
dying down, no more need for wood.

III

The Day Cornelius Ryan Came to the House
to Interview My Father for *The Last Battle*

It was a Thursday. April. My mother hurried home from work
to fix roast beef, potatoes, green beans with corn

and biscuits from a can she popped against the counter,
to see us children with spelling words copied

and book reports written, our faces washed and school clothes
changed to Sunday dresses and freshly ironed shirts,

to set the table with an extra plate, using the china
edged with blue lace, and the silver, not the stainless

forks and spoons she'd ordered from cereal boxes.
My father arrived home, whistling, kissed my mother

behind her ear, and brought his uniform from the bedroom closet.
He would have worn it but my mother mumbled

dry rot and *moth balls,* so instead
he hauled out his medals, scrapbooks and

photographs and spread them across the coffee table
and unfolded a bridge table so Cornelius Ryan

could open the maps and trace the red ink line
from Isigny to Magdeburg.

It was 1965. Our father didn't look to us like a hero.
Every night after supper he fell asleep in the recliner.

The hair that ringed his balding head was soft and gray.
He wore Bermuda shorts to mow the yard and puttered around

on Saturdays watering azaleas and building rock walls.
For dessert he would chunk butter with grape jelly,

smear it on white bread, then pour coffee from his cup
in the saucer and, to my mother's horror, slurp it gone.

Do not do that when Cornelius Ryan comes, she said
for the last time at breakfast that morning, and he smiled.

That evening, Cornelius Ryan, a large man with glasses
and a deep voice, spilled gravy on the chair cushion,

took second helpings of everything, even biscuits,
then settled in the living room with my father

until long after the dishes were cleared, long after
we children went to bed. I fell asleep

to the click-click-clicking of his tape recorder
as it looped in circles, capturing my father's stories.

It doesn't matter what really happened that night.
It doesn't matter if the blue-laced china and good silver

were at my grandmother's house not ours,
if the maps, the journals, the photographs

remained in their boxes until mildew ravaged them.
It doesn't matter how late Cornelius Ryan stayed

or how long the blue smoke from his cigarettes lingered.
In the morning, I woke to a clattering in the kitchen

and there was my father, aproned and humming,
stirring that day's oatmeal with a spoon.

Elaine

May 26, 1944

Dear Mama,

The other night a USO girl named Elaine
asked me where I was from
and when I said, *North Carolina*, she said,
Holy cow, I'm from Raleigh.
She gave me her telephone number,
said call her when this thing is over.
Then my buddy told me they say that to all the boys,
have the state capitals memorized, he said.
Asked me, *Did she sound like*
she was from our part of the world?
Come to think of it, she had some kind
of twang like her tongue was flapping
too much in her mouth. That's the story
of my 2-hour girlfriend Elaine, Mama.
So much for love in the good old US Army.

Love,
your boy Bill

Annie Gum Chum

Southampton, England, June 4, 1944

He calls her that because it's how they met,
her leaning against the brick wall of the pub,
skinny blue dress, cocked head rippled
with dark hair, eyes like shiny ale.
Got any gum, chum? Smile he fell into.
He happened to have some Juicy Fruit.

She works in a factory in the village
but won't tell him what kind.
Can't, say her bosses. Nobody knows
what they're waiting for. Nobody knows,
but something big stirs among them
like the hint of warm air.

He looks for her at the gate each afternoon
when girls spill out the factory doors,
walks with her to town for a mild and bitter.
Air raids have left her spooked.
When he scrapes his chair leg, she jumps
then settles, slides a Lucky Strike from his pack,

laughs. He watches as she pops her gum, lights up,
blows a smoke ring that rises and unravels.
She wants to take him home to meet her parents
but he doesn't even know her name.
Don't tell them anything and don't ask, his colonel advises.
Remember we're just passing through.

My Father Lands at Fox Red, Omaha Beach

June 12, 1944

The shells are finger-shaped,
driftwood quiet now as gulls that circle overhead,
his rifle cocked in case some renegade
German or crazed Carolina boy
still lurks in the dunes.

Pink waves lap his boots. He stumbles
on a testament swimming the surf.
A pair of shattered glasses.
Shells, shells, everywhere shells.
He scoops a fist of fleshy sand
and numbers breaths now buried
in this shore.

In the year to come,
he will walk this country, count
each KIA, each MIA, each wound,
even his. He will write of courage
as common as sniper fire,
of screams that cower beneath the gull's caw.
Honor, no honor, honor, no honor.

Years from now he will take
his daughter to another beach.
He will stand in white surf, waves pink with sun,
teach her to cast far beyond the swimmers.
She will learn the tug of fish from ocean's pull
and by her outstretched hand
will measure the small ones
and throw them back.

Finding Fox Red, 2014

One never paints violently enough.
        —Eugene Delacroix

You can't get there by car,
so we walk a narrow path of rocks
through grass and buttercups.
Ahead, the cliffs are brittle as old teeth.
Now and then a rain-washed gully
zigzags up to hedgerows sparkling from spring showers.
Overhead, early fog rises into sky,
a pattering of rain falls,
and waves lift and tumble over waves.
This stretch of sand is not marked by walkers or dogs.
Everything here welcomes us
except these hard stones at our feet
and the red, red sun, firing down between clouds.

My Son and I Fish for Bluegill

1

Where fish jump
at the edge of the lake,
concentric circles form
and grow perfectly toward
where we sit in webbed chairs
by the bank. My son's legs
flap like cane poles.
He tosses his line
to the bull's-eye and waits
for the bobber to go under.
It is June, the season when bluegill
swim to shallow water to spawn.

To catch a fish, I tell him,
you must be willing to wait.
You must be silent as air
and even when something tugs
your line you must hold
your breath in your fist.
Not everyone can do it.
So he molds himself to his chair,
eyes becoming the water,
distracted only by
one more acrobatic bream and
the gnat that visits his face.

2

I am ten at the cow pond.
My father beside me says, *Easy,*
easy, but my pudgy fist jerks
the wormless hook from water.
He says again, *Take your time.*
Where's the fire?" I squat on the

muddy bank, pink Sunday shorts
accepting Carolina clay,
skip dirt clods across the water,
scratch chigger bites,
keep one eye open for snakes.
These hands have not gripped cane
in twenty years, but some things
never change. Like the brown damp
smell of worms, the bite of sun that
bounces off water. *Did you and your
dad catch a lot of bluegill?*
my son asks. *Lots,* I say and
stare back through the years
unable to see just what we
pulled in or how many.

    3

Something tugs his line.
He tenses, poised.
Not yet, I whisper, *not yet.*
We stand without moving, then ease
to the water. A hundred feet out
a paddle boat laughs in circles.
Waves bounce toward us,
splash our feet. Seconds pass like years
clicked off in measured nibbles.
Sweat tickles down trees
like slow generations.

The bobber takes the lake.
Now, I say. *Now.*
Up, up, into the ancient,
breathed air, the turquoise fish
sails, strikes the flint of sun
and flames like blue fire
against this uncomplicated sky.

Hair Cutting

Bill straddles a metal chair,
arms folded across the top.
The company cook, who had a shop back home,
has brought out his clippers and scissors,

and men are lined up like for mess.
Tonight they'll play craps in circles
around their tents, betting cigarettes
and sticks of gum. In the morning

Bill will fill his helmet with water,
splash his cheeks, and shave
with the government issue razor
so small it fits in his palm.

A clean face can lift a man's spirits
as much as a full belly can.
He eyes the ground while the cook
clips the back of his neck. At his feet,

a mess of hair—blond, brown,
black, red, even a little gray—
little bits of hair
for wind and birds to claim.

Mess

July 1944

Bill slides his knife down the inside edge of the can,
scoops out a bladeful of beef stew, opens wide.
When he pulls it out, a line of blood
rises from the corner of his mouth.

That won't get you sent home,
someone calls over. And,
*Don't let your mama find out
the army taught you to eat with your knife.*

Laughter, even from him.
He's leaning on a fence post,
couple of sheep on a hilly slope as backdrop,
and he's thinking beans, soft and green,

not these mushy brown things they feed him,
fresh beef, not gravied lumps.
Two months now and just one bath,
hedgerows thicker than this stew,

and damned if every day another boy
doesn't get hit or go crazy with it all.
Late July and nothing but mud. Half the time
it rains, the other half, it rains more.

Still he gets up in the morning
surprised to be breathing. He's with
the best bunch of fellas ever was.
He's dropped some weight. They all have,

but he's stronger than ever, muscled with fear.
He laughs again, touches the corner of his mouth
with his thumb, stirs the muck called dinner,
slides another bladeful in.

Hedgerow

He knows about overgrown fields,
weeds dense and snaky,
blackberry bramble to his waist.
He knows about his mama's back hedge,
how its branches crisscross like fence wire,
how that little dog one time

got so gobbled up by honeysuckle and ivy,
they had to cut him out.
But he's never seen this kind of wall,
wide as a soldier is tall.
You could fit a whole family in there
or a boy with a herd of cows. Hell,

you could hide half a damn army,
and he wouldn't put it past
the sneaky sons of bitches.
Yesterday Captain Smith
was killed in a tree burst on the other side,
shrapnel raining down like slits of glass.

He lights this fuse himself, runs
before it blows—a hole wide enough
for a tank to pass through.
When the dust calms, he noses in,
remembering what Mama would say,
Something goes in there, it's as good as gone.

Children of Malmedy

Dec. 26, 1944—Red Cross stockings received by all men, containing socks, candy, apples, oranges, and nuts. All men give stockings to children of Malmedy whose families were killed in bombing.

Anaïs won't stop weeping.
She throws her stocking to the ground.
No! she says, brown hair flapping her face.
Little sister Matilde called Matty

searches among the families gathered
outside the cathedral. *Mama? Papa?*
Her little dog Helga burrows into her coat.
Snow climbs to her knees.

Bill sits on the waist-high wall beside Anaïs,
his arm draped around her shoulder like a shawl.
He feels the tremble of her tears,
cups his hand around her shoulder, squeezes.

If he had a daughter he would want her to be Anaïs
with her dark, intentional eyes,
mouth fixed in sorrow, someone
to love him so much, refuse to say he's gone.

Matty comes over, lays her head on his knee.
Poor Anny, she says. In her hand,
a peppermint stick, a green sock
stuffed in her pocket like a fist.

My Son Comes Home

He brings with him the ripe scent of summer,
unwashed, and a white bag of peaches he bought
at a roadside stand east of Raleigh

when he knew he'd be late and remembered
how much we love them, fresh-picked from trees
and so sweet their tender flesh trembles.

It has been six weeks since he left,
car packed, map unfolded across the passenger seat,
headed alone to a job across state, 18, on his own

for the first time. Now when he steps from the car
I am startled by the deep cast of his face,
the three-day beard that shades his cheeks.

We have grilled burgers to celebrate his return.
We gather at the table, passing awkwardness
among us like mayonnaise and tomatoes.

As he and his father talk baseball, war,
the market's ups and downs, it is all I can do
not to leap from my seat and take him in my arms.

Instead I gather him in with my eyes—
his large hands, the dark hairs curling up from knuckles,
chest, neck, shoulders, chin. He sees me, pulls free,

pushes back from the table, says,
How about dessert? At the faucet he turns
three soft peaches in his palms, washing,

and with a sharp knife, begins to trim,
the blade slipped beneath skin,
loose peels falling to the sink.

At the Abdij Rolduc after Being Hit by Shrapnel Fire

The chapel tower rises to the sky in prayer.
Mornings before dawn the monks begin to sing,
first the low murmur of earth rumbling

then a warbly welcome
like the Methodist church back home.
He watches from his window

as they pass through the courtyard,
long robes winging just above ground.
When the sun rises, soldiers drill in formation,

their steps weary with unfinished war.
The wound on his back rages.
Nurses with warm hands tend the bandages

that wrap his waist. At night, in the arms
of this old abbey, he dreams deep fields of green,
his mother's garden, its early squash, late corn.

In this welt of early winter,
his men on the line, he can't heal fast enough.
He tries to stand, falls to his knees.

The Death of Col. McCollum

Two yards from where the body lay,
Bill found his wallet, splayed open
to the photo of a woman standing in snow,
baby in her left arm, her right hand clutching

the fist of a small girl pressed into her waist.
On the back in slanted script,
Waiting here for you. Love forever.
His helmet had rolled off and was lying

in leaves not far from the river bank
they'd crossed earlier that day
as mortar fire shattered around them.
Bill pulled the dog tags, cursing.

What any of them would do now,
he couldn't say. He cried, blamed himself,
said he should've gone too, could've at least
hunted down the son of a bitch that got him.

Now he fires at everything that moves—
a rustle in the brush, a rabbit, a bird,
wind stirring. Hours ticking off
till everything he knows is gone.

A Sparrow Hangs by His Neck at My Feeder

He is not dead when I find him,
his marble-sized head caught
in a feast of seeds, neck twisted
sideways in the hole, his fat,
full belly trying desperately to fly
out of this mess and back to the flock
that has been idling at my kitchen window
all morning. I am as panicked
as he is when I finger his body,
talking in my soft mother voice, *Be still.*
Be still. Trust me. I lift the feeder
from the shepherd's crook and begin
to unbuild it. Over and over he opens
his wings, flapping, legs kicking, then quiets.

I can't let myself think what I fear:
that when he is loose, his round head
will flop against his chest like wet clay.
I lift off the cap, undo the base,
seed spilling everywhere across
the brick step and onto the pine needles
where I am kneeling, the bead
of his eyes shooting in every direction.
His mouth opens and closes like a baby's.
I beat the hollow feeder hard
against the ground. On the third hit,
he tumbles free. Then lifting, whole into sky,
his zig-zag straightens and blends
into the ordinary multitude of the living.

My Son Tells Me Goodbye

Hours before my plane home, he invites me
swimming. Towels, books, sunscreen, two beers
stuffed in the straw basket on the bicycle's handlebars.

He says, *Follow me*, and I do, across
four lanes of 6th Avenue, through the quiet
neighborhood of bungalows, over the drawbridge

to the beach. I watch the steady bobbing
of his white fedora, hands signaling turns
right or left, the occasional glance back

for cars or to make sure I'm still there.
Low tide, high noon. A fat bulldog tiptoes
across the sandbar, shakes water from his paws.

Three young girls and a soaked poodle are splayed
across blankets. The Florida water is clear as a lens.
We don goggles and plunge to the bottom,

scouring for fish or tiny shells he stores in pockets.
For an hour or more, we dive, surface, dive, surface.
She thinks I'm crazy for liking this, he says

of the woman he loves, and laughs. Back in our chairs,
we talk about nothing in particular
as though he still lives in the upstairs bedroom

and I'll see him again in the morning.
At last, we climb back on bikes, retrace our route
to his place where she is waiting.

From the doorway I watch how easily
he greets her, scoops up the red cat
for a kiss, reaches in his cabinet for a glass.

The Dance

Magdeburg, Germany

I have not yet been born to you
and you are nobody's father
when you step from the photograph

and take my hand. Behind us the green Elbe
pushes forward to the North Sea,
and trees rustle against an easy breeze.

Your boots shuffle beside my sandaled feet.
Your helmet tips my brown hair.
It doesn't matter that you are a boy my son's age

or that we are both so far from home.
I have followed you across four countries.
I have put my feet on the hard ground

of Eben-Emael where you put yours,
I have waited on the banks of the Wurm River
and watched for you to cross,

I have leap-frogged across this country
behind your leap-frogging.
Here, now, on this river, I have found you.

You don't know my mother
but I can tell you about her dark hair,
her body thin as a pencil, even to the end.

I can tell you about the mill, about our old dog King,
your brothers and sisters, and mine.
There is so much I have to tell you.

I can tell you everything.
Shush, you say, *shush*,
and touch, to my lips, your finger.

At the Butterfly Garden

We have just come through the double
entry doors when a scalloped lacewing
lights on my son's shoulder and pauses,
his wings opening and closing like hello.
My son laughs, offers his thumb as a stoop,
but the lacewing lifts into the bougainvillea,
circles among pink blossoms, and is lost
in the ordinariness of this extraordinary enclosure.
I have come for a long weekend to the home
my son shares with the woman he loves, their affection
made strong by distance and years and now
the constancy of every day. After a breakfast
of eggs and red oranges, we idle here among
teal and yellow finches, palm-sized hummingbirds
with beaks the size of fingers, lorikeets
that land on our arms and feed from our hands.
Tigers, blue morphos, zebras, daggerwings,
and swallowtails crisscross in soft threads.
We witness the emergence of a red piano key
from his crusty pupa, damp wings unfolding.
There is no hurry here in the gardens. Other families
visiting this tropical world weave easily along paths,
as amazed as we are by small miracles
of transformation. When I slow to study
the passion flowers, my son walks ahead,
his arm at her waist, sometimes brushing
a cheek, a misplaced hair, sometimes glancing
back to where I follow at a distance.

Notes

The epigraph by Henry Beston is from *The Outermost House: A Year of Life on the Great Beach of Cape Cod*, published in 1928 by Doubleday, Doran, and Co.

"Blue Star Mothers." The Blue Star Mothers, Inc. was formed in 1942 to support mothers of men and women in active service during the war. The custom was to hang a banner called a "Service Flag" in the window for each son or daughter currently serving. A blue star on the banner indicated that the soldier was still alive; upon death, a gold star was sewn over the blue.

The epigraph for "Diphtheria Outbreak, August 1898" was the common descriptor of diphtheria, the leading cause of death in children prior to the 1920's. As the "Report of the Lancet Sanitary Commission on Diphtheria: Its History, Progress, Symptoms, and Treatment" further explains, "As the access of suffocation is felt, the poor child turns from side to side, throws its arms into the air, clutches its mother violently, and struggles furiously to gain breath, then falls exhausted into bed. . . ." (*The Lancet*, Feb. 12, 1859, p. 169).

"Eastern Cherokee Application #13598" is based on the actual Eastern Cherokee application file #13598 and the included correspondence of Hannah Sharpe Presnell, my grandmother, as part of the Guion Miller Roll of 1909.

"Letters Home" is from the letters of 1st Sgt. Ernest E. Bunting to his wife, Wanda Robbins Bunting, my grandparents, Aug. 21, 1918–Oct. 6, 1918.

"How to Cuss in French" was a phrase scribbled on the cover of my father's 1928 French grammar textbook, *Elements of French* by Jacob Greenberg, A.M. (Charles E. Merrill Company, 1930), above the proper title, which was marked out. The owner's name, scrawled on the first page of the book, is "Billy Presnell."

"Back Home" is the almost exact wording from a letter written by 1st Sgt. Bill Presnell, my father, to his mother, Hannah Sharpe Presnell, date not given.

"What Flutters" is based on a true story about Company K, 30th Infantry Division, and the breaking of the Hindenburg line, Sept. 29, 1918.

"The Day Cornelius Ryan Came to the House to Interview My Father for *The Last Battle*." Cornelius Ryan did, in fact, interview my father for *The Last Battle*. Whether or not he visited the house is unknown. My father is quoted on p. 285 of *The Last Battle* (Simon and Schuster, 1966).

"Annie Gum Chum" is based on a letter from my father to his mother, dated June 4, 1944; a photograph of an English woman in my father's war scrapbook with the caption, "Any Gum Chum"; and the big band hit song, "Have Ya Got Any Gum, Chum," written by Murray Kane in 1944 and recorded by the Glenn Miller Orchestra in 1945. The words refer to the popular phrase spoken by British children to American soldiers, who would respond with gifts of Chiclets, Spearmint, Doublemint, and Juicy Fruit gum.

"My Father Lands at Fox Red, Omaha Beach" and "Finding Fox Red, 2014" are based on information taken from my father's journal, p. 25, and the return to the site by his children.

"Children of Malmedy" epigraph is from my father's journal, p. 31.

"The Death of Col. McCollum" is from a photograph in my father's scrapbook, and the death is also recorded on p. 9 and described on p. 28 of his journal. Lt. Col. Paul W. McCollum of Wentworth, NC, died on Oct. 6, 1944. He left behind a wife but no children.

"The Dance" is from a photograph of my father at the Elbe River in Magdeburg, Germany, and comes with many thanks to retired Lt. Frank Towers, who served beside my father from 1944-45 in the 30th Infantry Division and provided the photograph. Many thanks also go to Jürgen Ladebeck, who was able to pinpoint the exact location where the photograph was taken.

Barbara Presnell is the author of five collections of poetry, including *Piece Work*, which won the Cleveland State University Poetry Center First Book Prize and was adapted for stage by the Touring Theatre of North Carolina. She has been awarded fellowships from the North Carolina Arts Council, the Kentucky Arts Council, and the Kentucky Foundation for Women, and has held residencies at Willapa Bay, Wildacres Retreat, the Virginia Center for the Creative Arts, and Soapstone, Inc. A native of Asheboro, North Carolina, she teaches at the University of North Carolina at Charlotte and lives in Lexington, North Carolina, with her husband, Bill Keesler.

Cover artist and Lexington, North Carolina, native Lee Hall has pursued careers as artist, educator, and writer. Her paintings allow us to share her love for subtle shapes, variety in texturing, and civilized muted color relationships. Her works are poetic landscapes, many deriving from the tradition of abstractions produced by meditations on nature, a tradition which encompasses the painters of the Sung Dynasty as well as modernist John Marin and abstract expressionist Helen Frankenthaler.

Throughout her academic career, Hall painted and exhibited her work, most notably at the Betty Parsons Gallery. The recipient of numerous prestigious awards, including the Childe Hassam Purchase Award from the American Academy of Arts and Letters in 1977, her work can be found in museum collections such as the Greenville Museum, the Hudson River Museum, the Montclair Art Museum, and New York University, among others.

CPSIA information can be obtained at www.ICGtesting.com
Printed in the USA
BVOW03s1310190816

459401BV00002B/4/P